THE STORY BEHIND

SKYSCRAPERS

Sean Stewart Price

Heinemann Library
Chicago, Illinois

www.heinemannraintree.com
Visit our website to find out
more information about
Heinemann-Raintree books.

To order:
☎ Phone 888-454-2279
💻 Visit www.heinemannraintree.com
to browse our catalog and order online.

©2009 Heinemann Library
an imprint of Capstone Global Library, LLC
Chicago, Illinois

Edited by Louise Galpine, Abby Colich, and Laura Knowles
Designed by Philippa Jenkins and Artistix
Original illustrations © Capstone Global Library, LLC 2009
Illustrated by Phil Gleaves/Specs Art
Picture research by Mica Brancic and Elaine Willis
Originated by Modern Age Repro House Ltd
Printed in in China by CTPS

13 12 11 10 09
10 9 8 7 6 5 4 3 2 1

Library of Congress Cataloging-in-Publication Data
Price, Sean Stewart.
The story behind skyscrapers / Sean Stewart Price.
    p. cm. -- (True stories)
Includes bibliographical references and index.
ISBN 978-1-4329-2349-5 (hc)
1. Skyscrapers--Juvenile literature. I. Title.
TH1615.P75 2008
720'.483--dc22
                2008043411

Acknowledgments
The author and publishers are grateful to the following for
permission to reproduce copyright material: akg-images
p. 7 (© James Morris); Alamy p. 27 (© Tibor Bognar);
Corbis pp. 6 (© Jose Fuste Raga), 8 (© Jose Fuste Raga), 9
(© Bettmann), 11 (© Daniella Nowtiz), 12 (© Ausloeser/
zefa), 14 (© Walter Hodges), 15 (© Bettmann), 17
(© Bettmann), 20 top (Reuters/© Sean Adair), 20 bottom
(© dbox for the Lower Manhattan Development Corporation),
24 (© Andrew Holbrooke), 25 (Reuters/© Anwar Mirza),
26 (© Paul Hardy); Getty Images pp. 4 (© Guy Vanderelst),
19 (© Louie Psihoyos); Photolibrary.com pp. 10
(© Imagestate RM/Jeremy Walker), 16 (© age fotostock/
Javier Larrea), 21 (© Digital Vision), 22 (© Panorama
Media); Press Association p. 23 (© AP Photo/Alan
Welner); Shutterstock p. iii (© Losevsky Pavel); The Kobal
Collection p. 5 (© RKO).

Cover photograph of a skyscraper reproduced with
permission of Getty Images (Taxi Japan).

Contents

■ **Soaring into the Sky** 4

■ **Early Skyscrapers**. 6

■ **Planning and Building a Skyscraper**. 10

■ **The Dangers of Building High** . . 16

■ **Skyscrapers Today**. 22

■ *Timeline*. 28

■ *Glossary*. 30

■ *Find Out More* 31

■ *Index* 32

Some words are shown in bold, **like this**. You can find out what they mean by looking in the glossary.

Soaring into the Sky

▲ Today, people are building skyscrapers taller than ever before.

▲ Today, people are building skyscrapers taller than ever before.

Reaching for the right word ✔

The word *skyscraper* originally applied to sailing ships. It was used to describe the tallest sail on the ship.

The next time you are near tall buildings, look up. It is easy to see why people call them skyscrapers. These buildings look like they touch the sky. People looking up cannot believe they go so high.

Skyscrapers certainly touch our lives. They give us places to live, shop, and work. Some people say that a true skyscraper must be at least 20 **stories** (floors) high. But there is no agreed-upon minimum height. A skyscraper is just a very tall building.

Skyscrapers are part of our everyday world. But skyscrapers have been around just over 100 years. In the late 1800s, a building 10 stories high could amaze people. Today, the tallest skyscrapers soar more than 100 stories.

Skyscrapers will soon go much higher. There may be buildings that reach 1.6 kilometers (1 mile) into the air. Building any skyscraper takes thousands of people. It also takes expert knowledge. Keep reading to see how skyscrapers are made and how they affect our world.

King Kong ✔

Many people are afraid of great heights. Hollywood likes to use that fear to scare moviegoers. A hero like Spiderman or Batman saves someone from falling off a building. But the most famous skyscraper movie is *King Kong*. The 1933 and 2005 versions of *King Kong* showed the giant ape climbing the Empire State Building in New York City.

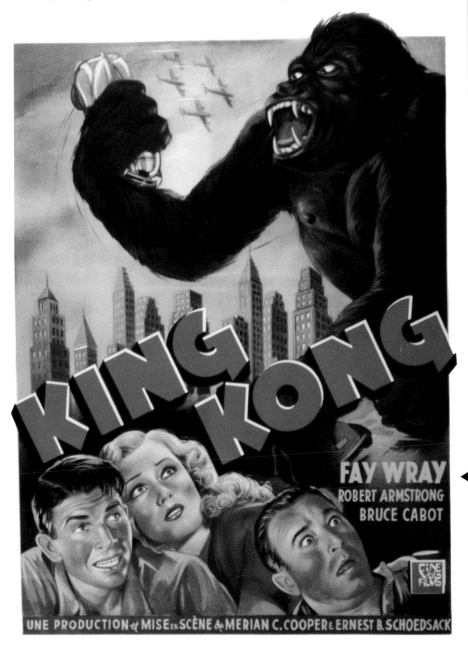

◀ This is a poster for the 1933 movie *King Kong*. The movie made the Empire State Building even more famous than before.

Early Skyscrapers

▲ **The pyramids of Egypt were the skyscrapers of the ancient world.**

People have always tried to build bigger and bigger buildings. In ancient times, the largest buildings ever made were Egypt's pyramids. Built around 2550 BCE, the Great Pyramid of Khufu was the world's tallest structure. It was 147 meters (481 feet) tall. Unlike modern skyscrapers, the pyramids were not places to live and work. They were built as tombs for Egypt's pharaohs, or kings.

2550 BCE
The Great Pyramid of Khufu, in Egypt, is built. It is the world's tallest building.

6

3000 BCE   2000 BCE   1000 BCE

Later people tried to create buildings bigger than the pyramids. Christians built many **cathedrals** (large churches). These were seen as a way of reaching for God.

Too heavy or too weak

The pyramids remained the world's tallest buildings until a tall **spire** was built on Lincoln Cathedral in England in 1311. The spire collapsed during a storm in 1549. Materials would not let people build very high. Buildings used mostly stone, brick, and wood. Brick and stone are very heavy. People who built too high found that brick and stone buildings collapsed. Wood was lighter. But it was not as strong and caught fire easily. New inventions were needed to make skyscrapers possible.

◀ Visitors come from all over the world to see the Leaning Tower of Pisa in Italy.

1284	**1311–1549**
The Leaning Tower of Pisa is completed.	Lincoln Cathedral, England, is the world's tallest building until its spire falls down.

0   1000   2000

7

An age of iron and steel

In 1889 the French government built the Eiffel Tower in Paris. The tower's **architect** (designer) was named Gustave Eiffel. The Eiffel Tower was 312 meters (1,024 feet) tall. That made it the tallest manmade structure at the time. The Eiffel Tower was built as part of a celebration. In 1889 France celebrated 100 years since the French Revolution of 1789.

The Eiffel Tower is not a building that people work or live in. But it helped pave the way for buildings like skyscrapers. The Eiffel Tower was made of more than 18,000 pieces of iron. Iron had been around for centuries. In the 1700s, iron makers found new ways to make it stronger and lighter. They began to use iron to build bridges and buildings. In the 1850s, they also began using steel. It is a combination of iron and carbon. Steel is even stronger and lighter than iron.

▲ The Eiffel Tower in Paris is no longer the tallest manmade object but it still attracts visitors from all over the world.

1700s
Iron makers find new ways to make iron lighter and stronger.

1850s
Steel begins to be used in the construction of buildings and bridges.

1800

The first skyscraper

Five years earlier, in 1884, U.S. architect William Le Baron Jenney designed the very first skyscraper. It was the 10-**story** Home Insurance Building in Chicago. As a young man, Jenney visited islands in the Pacific Ocean. He saw that people there used lightweight wooden frames to build. These frames stayed upright even in huge storms. Jenney copied the frames for his buildings. But he made them out of steel. Jenney's—and Eiffel's—designs were widely copied to make tall buildings. Skyscrapers began popping up, especially in U.S. cities.

◀ By the time this photograph of the Home Insurance Building was taken in the 1920s, taller buildings had been built around the "first skyscraper."

1884
U.S. architect William Le Baron Jenney designs the first skyscraper, the Home Insurance Building in Chicago.

1889
The Eiffel Tower is built in Paris. It is taller than any other manmade structure at the time.

late 1800s
Architects begin to create more skyscrapers throughout the world, especially in U.S. cities.

1900

Planning and Building a Skyscraper

▲ The wind that blows these flags also pushes against tall buildings. Skyscrapers are built to stay strong in these winds.

Important decisions have to be made about where and how to build skyscrapers. **Architects** and **engineers** make these decisions. These decisions take into account the following:

Weight

Architects and engineers have to think about the weight of the building. They must also consider the weight of the objects – including people – inside the building. If they do not, the building could become damaged over time.

Soil

The ground the skyscraper is built on is important. Much of New York City's ground is solid rock. It is very stable. It allows many skyscrapers to be built. But most skyscrapers are built on dirt. Dirt is not as stable. Builders must construct deep **foundations**. That keeps the building from leaning or sinking.

Temperature

Changing temperatures can cause metals, glass, and concrete to expand and shrink. Architects and engineers must take this into account. They have to give the building room to change with the seasons.

Wind

Winds are strong high up in the air. Most skyscrapers are built to bend in a high wind, like a tall tree. Some skyscrapers might sway eight to ten centimeters (three or four inches). Without this, the building would weaken dangerously.

Vibrations

Vibrations shake a skyscraper every minute. People walk. Machines hum. Cars park in garages. All this has to be thought through.

> **Material world** ✓
>
> Architects and engineers are always looking for lighter, stronger building materials. These reduce a skyscraper's massive weight and make it safer. But sometimes new inventions cause problems. During construction in 1973, windows started popping out of Boston's John Hancock Building. The 227-kilogram (500-pound) windows smashed on the sidewalk below. The windows were made using a new, untested process. They did not hold up to changes in wind and temperature.

▶ **All 10,344 windows of Boston's John Hancock Building had to be replaced by the time it opened in 1976.**

Designing a giant

The second stage in building a skyscraper is the design. This process can be done in months. But it often takes years.

With help from engineers, architects come up with a **blueprint** (plan). Construction companies follow the blueprints when they put the building together.

In the past, blueprints were made up of lines on blue paper. Today, the plans for buildings are done mainly using computers. Computers are faster than making old-fashioned blueprints. They also show more clearly how the finished building will look.

Building tall

There are three ways to build a skyscraper:

1 Many columns

A **column** is an upright support. It is usually made of stone or concrete. A lot of older skyscrapers, such as the Empire State Building (finished 1931), are supported by many columns throughout the building.

Pluses: Very strong.

Minuses: Columns take up a lot of room.

2 Hollow tube

With hollow tube construction, the main support comes from the building's outside walls. New York City's World Trade Center (finished 1971; see page 20) used this design.

Pluses: Allows for a lot of office space.

Minuses: Stronger walls mean there is less room for big windows.

3 Inner core

When a building uses an inner core, the main support comes from a concrete tube that runs up the center of the building. It supports the building the way a backbone supports a human being. Most modern skyscrapers are built this way.

Pluses: Gives lots of room and allows for large windows.

Minuses: The core alone might not support the building well in an area prone to earthquakes or storms.

▶ These diagrams show the three main skyscraper structures and how their supports look from above.

Many columns

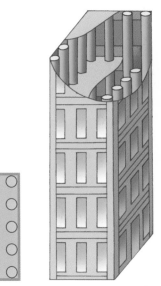

Hollow tube

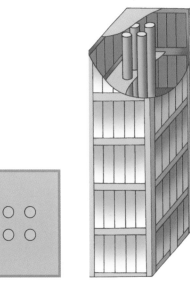

Inner core

13

▲ Construction
workers put up
a horizontal steel
beam while building
a skyscraper in
California, USA.

Making a skyscraper, step-by-step

The construction stage of building a skyscraper also
takes many years. It is usually done in nine steps:

1 Clear land. Trees and old buildings must be removed.

2 Dig a hole for the foundation. Ideally, the foundation
   is laid on bedrock. The bedrock is the solid layer of
   rock under the surface dirt. If bedrock cannot
   be reached, the building must rest on firm,
   stable ground.

3 Install footings. Footings are big pads. They are
   found at the base of the skyscraper. They spread out
   the building's weight in the bottom of the pit.

4 Put up vertical support beams (beams that run up and down). These beams bear much of the building's weight.

5 Put up horizontal steel beams (beams that run side to side). These help hold the building together.

6 Put up outside walls. These support the building and protect it from wind and weather.

7 Put up interior walls. These also keep out wind and weather.

8 Install electric wiring, phones, and plumbing. Wires and pipes usually run up the center of the building, near the core.

9 Furnish offices or apartments and move in.

Elisha Otis

Elevators have been used since ancient times. Elevators were once pulled up and down on ropes. If the rope snapped, the elevator fell. In 1852 the U.S. engineer Elisha Otis created the elevator brake. Then, if the rope snapped, Otis's brake brought the elevator safely to a halt. Elevators—and Otis's brake—made skyscrapers possible.

◀ In this 1853 drawing, Elisha Otis shows a crowd of people how his elevator brake works.

The Dangers of Building High

▲ Safety nets help
to stop people and
objects falling onto
the streets when
skyscrapers are
being built.

On March 15, 2008, a New York City work crew was building a skyscraper. The workers were using a construction **crane**. It is used to lift and move heavy weights. Suddenly, the crane fell. It killed seven people and hurt several others.

Problems like this are common with skyscrapers. All construction jobs can be dangerous. But tall buildings pose extra dangers. Winds on upper floors are very strong. They can help push over cranes. High winds also cause workers to fall.

Avoiding accidents

Cities have rules to protect workers. In New York City, safety nets are put around skyscrapers being built. These catch workers who fall. They also protect people on the streets from falling objects. But nets cannot always catch every person or object that falls.

Other cities worldwide also have skyscraper accidents. Many workers must dangle from high places to do their work. The same is true of the people who wash windows. The number of skyscrapers worldwide has jumped in recent years. So, the number of skyscraper accidents has risen, too.

Taking big risks ✔

Safety was not as important in the past as it is now. The people who planned the Empire State Building in the 1920s thought that one worker would die for each floor of the building. If they had been right, 102 people would have died. Luckily, only about five were killed. But accidents were more common back then.

▼ These construction workers in 1932 are having lunch. They are dangling high above New York City!

Mixing the old with the new ✓

People in Taiwan follow many Chinese traditions. One of them is the belief in feng shui (pronounced "fung shway"). It is a very old type of "earth magic." Feng shui has certain rules. For instance, a door in the wrong place might welcome evil spirits. A wall in the wrong place might block good spirits. Taipei 101 follows the rules of feng shui.

▼ This diagram shows the main damper in Taipei 101. The red arrows show the movement of the damper in an earthquake.

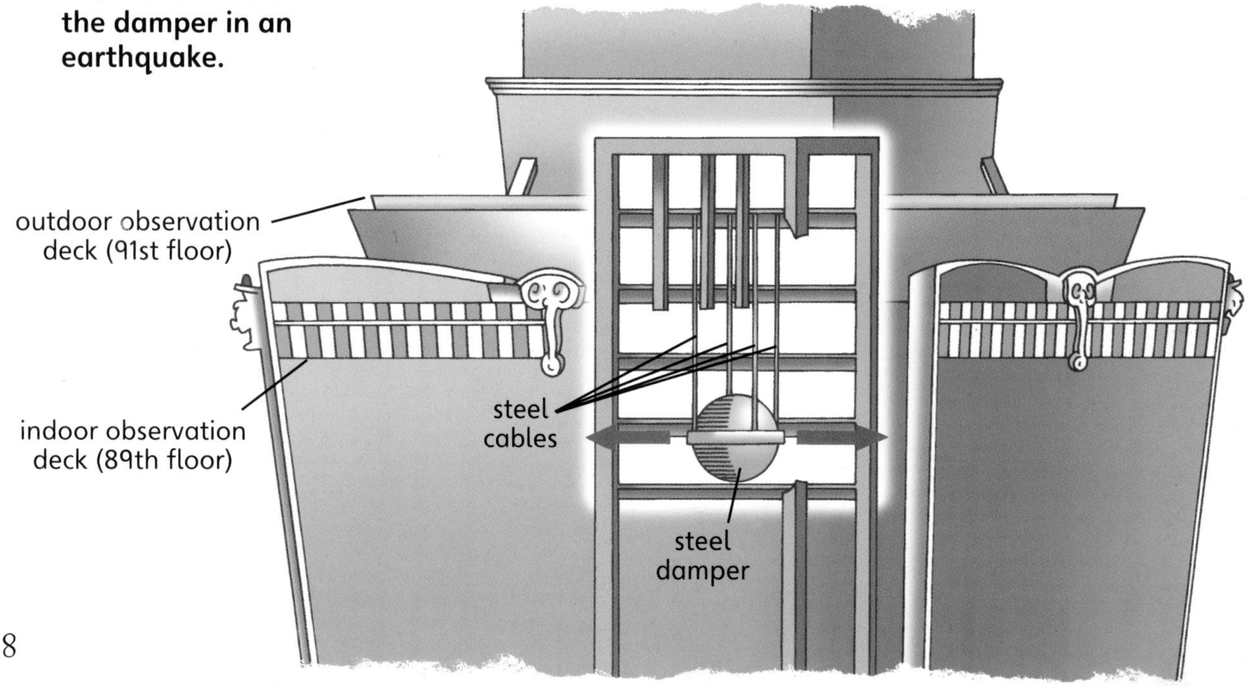

Natural disasters

In 2002 an earthquake hit Taipei, Taiwan. At the time, the building called Taipei 101 was under construction. The quake caused cranes to fall. Five people died. All work stopped on the huge skyscraper for three months. But the building itself was fine. It was finished in 2004. From 2004 to 2007, it was the world's tallest building—until Burj Dubai in the United Arab Emirates was built (see page 24 and 25).

Like all skyscrapers, Taipei 101 must fight the forces of nature. Earthquakes and high winds are two of the biggest threats to skyscrapers. On most modern buildings, **architects** combat them using **dampers**. A damper is a giant weight. When a building sways one way, the damper moves the other. This helps keep the building in balance. Computers help monitor the damper.

Taipei 101 has three huge dampers. One of them is the world's biggest damper. It weighs 662 tonnes (728 tons). That is the same weight as about 90 double-decker buses. In 2008 an earthquake hit nearby China. Taipei 101's dampers swayed back and forth a lot during the quake. They kept the building from suffering damage.

outdoor observation deck (91st floor)

indoor observation deck (89th floor)

steel cables

steel damper

▶ Taipei 101 has 101 floors above ground and another five underground.

▶ This photograph was taken just after an airplane was crashed into the World Trade Center, New York.

September 11, 2001

The biggest skyscraper disaster occurred in New York City on September 11, 2001. A group of men hijacked (forcefully took over) large airplanes. They crashed two of those planes into the twin towers of the World Trade Center.

The plane crashes spilled flaming gasoline throughout the buildings. Both fires became extremely hot. The fire caused metal supports to weaken. Within two hours, both buildings had caved in. More than 2,700 people were killed.

Freedom Tower

In 2006 workers began building the replacement for the World Trade Center buildings. It is one building called Freedom Tower. At 541 meters (1,776 feet), it will be the tallest building in the United States.

◀ The Freedom Tower is scheduled to be completed in 2013.

The building's designers learned from the 2001 attacks. They created extra-wide stairs. These will allow people to escape danger easily. Much of the glass will resist explosions better. There are also special stairways. They are just for police and firefighters. They allow emergency workers to climb up and down faster when they are trying to help people.

Destroying skyscrapers on purpose ✔

Like any other building, skyscrapers get old. People need to replace them. Tearing down a skyscraper piece-by-piece would take a lot of time and money. Instead, the buildings are **imploded** (caved in). The old building is totally emptied out. Then explosives are placed at key areas on the bottom floors. The explosions destroy the building's supports. That causes the skyscraper to fall straight down, rather than toppling sideways.

▼ This series of photos shows an old skyscraper being imploded.

Skyscrapers Today

▲ In the busy cities of Hong Kong, many people rely on buses and trains for transport.

The World Trade Center attacks worried people. Many doubted that skyscrapers had a future. They were seen as too dangerous.

But skyscraper construction has increased since 2001. Skyscrapers greatly change their surroundings. They create **population density**. That means many people live and work in a small area. So, there is less room for cars and big houses. Most cities with many skyscrapers rely heavily on buses and trains to move people around.

Sometimes loud and crowded

Life amid skyscrapers can have drawbacks. Sounds like police sirens tend to echo off tall buildings. So, living in those cities can be loud. It is also crowded. Many people compete for the same homes and jobs.

But the need for greater population density is becoming more important. Earth's population is growing rapidly. Today, there are about 6.5 billion people. By 2050 there will probably be around 9 billion. The number of skyscrapers is likely to keep rising.

Running to the top ✓

Each year, the Empire State Building hosts a special race. Runners must go up 1,576 steps, or 86 **stories**. The record for running that distance is 9 minutes, 33 seconds.

Climbing the hard way ✓

Climbing up the outside of skyscrapers is both dangerous and illegal. But many people like the challenge. In 2008 three people climbed up the new 52-story New York Times Building (finished 2007) in New York City. In 1974 Frenchman Philippe Petit took up a bigger challenge. He walked on a high wire between the two World Trade Center buildings for more than an hour.

▼ Philippe Petit used a special cane to balance while walking on a high wire between the World Trade Center buildings, New York.

What goes into a skyscraper?

In 2009 Burj Dubai (pronounced "burzsh doo-BYE") became the tallest building in the world. It is in the United Arab Emirates. The super-tall skyscraper has 160 stories. What did it take to build Burj Dubai? Here are a few fast facts:

- The building contains 230,000 cubic meters (300,000 cubic yards) of concrete. That weighs as much as 100,000 elephants.

- The outside walls contain 11 hectares (27.5 acres) of metal and glass. That would cover 25 football fields.

- Three window-washing units need three to four months to clean all the windows once.

▼ It took five years to build Burj Dubai. This photo shows it under construction in 2007.

- The tower can hold up to 35,000 people. But usually only about half that number work and live there.

- The tower uses up to 946,000 liters (250,000 gallons) of water per day.

- Double-decker elevators can carry 42 people at a time. They are the world's fastest, moving at 64 kilometers (40 miles) per hour.

- The tower contains the world's biggest shopping mall, with around 1,400 stores.

▲ Before Burj Dubai was built, this picture was made to show people what the skyscraper would look like.

Who decides the tallest of all?

The Council on Tall Buildings in Chicago lays down the rules for measuring skyscrapers. The council says that all buildings must be measured from the sidewalk level to the very top. The top can include **spires**. These are needle-shaped towers on top of many buildings (such as the Empire State Building). But it cannot include TV antennas or cell phone towers.

St. Mary Axe is a very different shape from any other skyscraper in London, England.

The future of skyscrapers

Years ago, most new skyscrapers looked alike. They were big boxes of glass and steel. Today, skyscrapers come in all shapes and sizes.

St. Mary Axe, London, United Kingdom (2003)

This 41-story building is shaped like a fruit called a gherkin, which is similar to a pickle. So, people call it the Gherkin. The building's outer walls curve in an unusual way. Yet none of the 5,500 triangles of glass in the outer wall is curved.

Bahrain World Trade Center, Bahrain (2007)

Many skyscrapers are going "green." That means they are built in ways to help protect the environment. This 50-story skyscraper was the first to build wind power into its design. About one-tenth of the building's electricity comes from three wind **turbines**. A turbine is a machine that spins to turn motion into energy. Many skyscrapers also use **solar panels**. They turn the sun's light into electricity.

China Central Television Headquarters, Beijing, China (2008)

This building is not a tower that goes straight up. Instead, it makes a giant, crooked loop that reaches 50 stories high. The loop has a meaning. It stands for the constant circle of gathering information and passing it on.

The Dynamic Tower, Dubai, United Arab Emirates (2010)

Architects are planning to build a new type of apartment building. Each of its 80 floors will slowly rotate, or turn, individually. A person who watches the sun rise in one room could watch it set in the same room. The tower's appearance will change every time a floor changes position.

▼ Bahrain World Trade Center was designed with three wind turbines to help make electricity.

Timeline

(These dates are often approximations.)

2550 BCE
The Great Pyramid of Khufu, in Egypt, is built. It is the world's tallest building.

3000 BCE · 2000 BCE

1600

1650

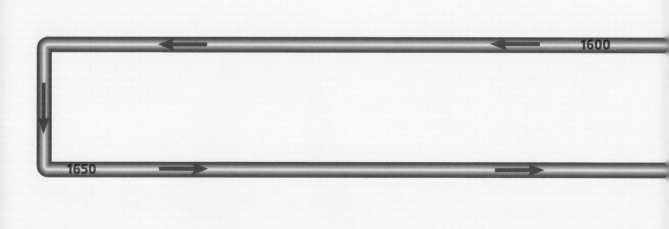

1800

1850s
Steel begins to be used in the construction of buildings and bridges.

1852
U.S. **engineer** Elisha Otis creates the elevator brake.

1884
U.S. **architect** William Le Baron Jenney designs the first skyscraper, the Home Insurance Building in Chicago.

1850

2004
Taipei 101, in Taipei, Taiwan, is completed and becomes the world's tallest building.

September 11, 2001
The World Trade Center in New York City is attacked and destroyed.

2000

2009
Burj Dubai, in the United Arab Emirates, becomes the world's tallest building.

2013
The Freedom Tower in New York City is projected to be completed.

2050

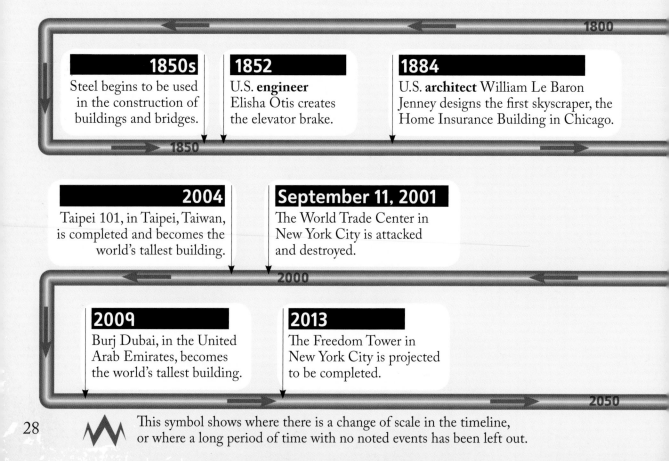

This symbol shows where there is a change of scale in the timeline, or where a long period of time with no noted events has been left out.

1000 BCE   **0**

1311–1549
Lincoln Cathedral, England, is the world's tallest building until its **spire** falls down.

1284
The Leaning Tower of Pisa is completed.

1000

1700s
Iron makers find new ways to make iron lighter and stronger.

1700

1750

1889
The Eiffel Tower is built in Paris. It is taller than any other manmade structure at the time.

late 1800s
Architects begin to create more skyscrapers throughout the world, especially in U.S. cities.

1900

1931
The Empire State Building is completed in New York City.

1950

Glossary

architect someone who designs buildings. An architect can work many years to design one skyscraper.

BCE meaning "before the common era." When this appears after a date, it refers to the time before the Christian religion began. BCE dates are always counted backwards.

blueprint building's printed design. Blueprints were once made on blue paper, but today they are done mostly on computers.

cathedral large church. Cathedrals were some of the world's tallest buildings until skyscrapers came along.

column upright support. Skyscrapers often use many columns.

crane piece of machinery used to lift and move heavy objects. Cranes are important during building construction.

damper giant weight. Dampers are used to keep skyscrapers from swaying too much in high winds or earthquakes.

engineer someone who uses scientific knowledge to solve problems. Engineers help design and build skyscrapers.

foundation building's base. The foundation must be strong or the building will weaken and perhaps fall.

implode collapse inward. Implosion is a method of destroying old skyscrapers.

population density many people living and working in a small area. Skyscrapers tend to increase population density.

solar panel large panel that absorbs the sun's rays. Solar panels help convert the sun's energy into electricity.

spire needle-shaped tower. Many skyscrapers have spires.

story floor of a building. Some people define skyscrapers as buildings with 20 stories or more.

turbine machine that spins to turn motion into energy. Wind turbines spin to turn the motion of the wind into electrical energy.

Find Out More

Books

Curlee, Lynn. *Skyscraper*. New York: Atheneum, 2007.

Hopkinson, Deborah. *Sky Boys: How They Built the Empire State Building*. New York: Schwartz & Wade, 2006.

Oxlade, Chris. *Building Amazing Structures: Skyscrapers*. Chicago: Heinemann Library, 2006.

Websites

This official website of Burj Dubai includes fun facts about the world's tallest building.
www.burjdubai.com

These two websites show how New York City is making the transition from the World Trade Center to the Freedom Tower.
www.wtc.com
www.pbs.org/wgbh/nova/wtc

This website provides a simple introduction to the world of skyscrapers.
www.allaboutskyscrapers.com/

This PBS website is the companion to the Building Big television series.
www.pbs.org/wgbh/buildingbig/skyscraper/index.html

Organizations

Skyscraper Museum
39 Battery Place
New York, N.Y. 10280

This private nonprofit museum started in 1996 and is dedicated to the study of tall buildings. Its exhibits help show how skyscrapers have changed daily life.

Index

accidents 17, 18
apartment buildings 27
architects 8, 9, 10, 11, 12, 18, 27

Bahrain World Trade Center 27
beams
    horizontal beams 15
    vertical support beams 15
bedrock 14
bell towers 7
blueprints 12
brick 7
building materials 7
    brick 7
    concrete 11, 13, 24
    glass 11, 21, 24, 26
    iron 8
    steel 8, 9, 14, 15
    stone 7
    wood 7, 9
Burj Dubai 18, 24-5

cathedrals 7
China Central Television Headquarters 27
climbing skyscrapers 23
columns 13
computer design 12
concrete 11, 13, 24
construction methods 13
    process 14–15
construction companies 12
construction workers 17
cranes 17, 18

dampers 18
dangers 16–21, 22
design 12–13
Dynamic Tower 27

earthquakes 13, 18
Egypt, Ancient 6
Eiffel Tower 8
electric wiring 15
electricity 27
elevators 15, 25
emergency workers 21
Empire State Building 5, 13, 17, 23, 25
engineers 10, 11

feng shui 18
footings 14
foundations 7, 10, 14
frames 9
France 8
Freedom Tower 20–1

glass 11, 21, 24, 26
Great Pyramid of Khufu 6
"green" skyscrapers 27

heights, fear of 5
high wire walking 23
hollow tube construction 13
Home Insurance Building 9
Hong Kong 22

implode 21
inner core 13
iron 8

John Hancock Building 11

King Kong 5

Le Baron Jenney, William 9
Leaning Tower of Pisa 7
Lincoln Cathedral 7

measuring skyscrapers 25

New York Times Building 23
noise 23

Otis, Elisha 15

plumbing 15
population density 22, 23
pyramids 6, 7

races 23
rock 10, 14

safety nets 16, 17
St. Mary Axe (Gherkin) 26
September 11, 2001 terrorist attacks 20
shopping malls 25
skyscrapers
    early skyscrapers 6-9
    heights 5, 24
    measuring 25
    original use of the word 4
    planning and building 10–15
    taking down 21
soil 7, 10
solar panels 27
spires 25
stairways 21
steel 8, 9, 14, 15
stone 7
stories 4, 24, 26, 27
storms 13
swaying 10, 11, 18

Taipei 101 18–19
Taiwan 18–19
taking down a skyscraper 21

temperature changes 11
towers 25
turbines 27

United Arab Emirates 24–5, 27
United Kingdom 7, 26
United States 5, 9, 10, 11, 13, 14, 15, 17, 20–1, 23

vibrations 11

walls
    interior 15
    outside 15
weight 10, 11
wind power 27
windows 11, 13
    washing 17, 24
winds 11, 17, 18
wood 7, 9
World Trade Center 13, 20, 22, 23